50 Premium Coconut Dish Ideas

By: Kelly Johnson

Table of Contents

- Coconut Crusted Shrimp
- Coconut Curry Chicken
- Coconut Mango Sticky Rice
- Coconut-Crusted Tofu
- Coconut Rice Pudding
- Coconut Shrimp Tacos
- Thai Coconut Soup (Tom Kha Gai)
- Coconut and Lime Chicken Skewers
- Coconut Cream Pie
- Coconut Avocado Salad
- Coconut Banana Pancakes
- Coconut-Lime Grilled Salmon
- Coconut-Curry Beef Stew
- Coconut Almond Macaroons
- Coconut-Sesame Grilled Scallops
- Coconut-Chocolate Truffles
- Coconut Sweet Potato Soup
- Coconut Yogurt Parfait
- Coconut Milk Ice Cream
- Coconut-Rice Stuffed Peppers
- Coconut-Cashew Chicken Stir-Fry
- Coconut-Maple Granola
- Coconut Cabbage Slaw
- Coconut and Mango Chutney
- Coconut-Lime Bars
- Coconut-Peanut Butter Smoothie
- Coconut Creamed Spinach
- Coconut-Curry Mussels
- Coconut Panna Cotta
- Coconut Date Energy Balls
- Coconut-Curry Hummus
- Coconut Shrimp with Pineapple Salsa
- Coconut Chicken Skewers with Peanut Sauce
- Coconut Chocolate Cake
- Coconut-Banana Smoothie

- Coconut Milk Risotto with Shrimp
- Coconut Creamed Corn
- Coconut-Chicken Satay
- Coconut-Peanut Stir-Fried Noodles
- Coconut-Pumpkin Soup
- Coconut-Cilantro Rice
- Coconut-Rosemary Lamb Chops
- Coconut Mousse with Raspberries
- Coconut Rice with Mango and Chia
- Coconut and Spinach Frittata
- Coconut Pineapple Rice
- Coconut-Chocolate Chip Cookies
- Coconut Baked Cod with Lime
- Coconut-Lavender Scones
- Coconut Lime Cheesecake

Coconut Crusted Shrimp

Ingredients:

- 1 lb large shrimp, peeled and deveined
- 1/2 cup flour
- 2 eggs, beaten
- 1 cup shredded coconut (sweetened or unsweetened)
- 1/2 cup panko breadcrumbs
- 1 teaspoon salt
- 1/2 teaspoon black pepper
- Vegetable oil for frying

Instructions:

1. Set up a dredging station with three shallow bowls: one with flour, one with beaten eggs, and one with a mixture of shredded coconut, panko breadcrumbs, salt, and pepper.
2. Dip each shrimp first in the flour, then in the egg, and finally coat in the coconut-panko mixture.
3. Heat oil in a frying pan over medium-high heat. Fry shrimp in batches for 2-3 minutes on each side until golden brown and crispy.
4. Drain on paper towels and serve with a dipping sauce of your choice.

Coconut Curry Chicken

Ingredients:

- 1 lb chicken breast or thighs, cubed
- 1 tablespoon vegetable oil
- 1 onion, chopped
- 2 cloves garlic, minced
- 1 tablespoon fresh ginger, minced
- 1 tablespoon red curry paste
- 1 can (14 oz) coconut milk
- 1/2 cup chicken broth
- 1 tablespoon fish sauce
- 1 tablespoon lime juice
- 1 tablespoon brown sugar
- Fresh cilantro for garnish
- Rice for serving

Instructions:

1. Heat oil in a large pan over medium heat. Add onions, garlic, and ginger, and sauté until soft and fragrant.
2. Add the curry paste and cook for another minute.
3. Stir in coconut milk, chicken broth, fish sauce, lime juice, and brown sugar. Bring to a simmer.
4. Add the chicken cubes to the pan and cook for 8-10 minutes until the chicken is cooked through.
5. Garnish with fresh cilantro and serve with rice.

Coconut Mango Sticky Rice

Ingredients:

- 1 cup sticky rice (or glutinous rice)
- 1 can (14 oz) coconut milk
- 1/4 cup sugar
- 1/4 teaspoon salt
- 1 ripe mango, peeled and sliced

Instructions:

1. Rinse the sticky rice in cold water until the water runs clear. Steam the rice for 20-25 minutes or until tender.
2. In a saucepan, combine coconut milk, sugar, and salt. Heat over low heat, stirring until the sugar dissolves.
3. Once the rice is done, transfer it to a bowl and pour the coconut milk mixture over it. Stir to combine and let it absorb the liquid for 10-15 minutes.
4. Serve the sticky rice with fresh mango slices on the side.

Coconut-Crusted Tofu

Ingredients:

- 1 block firm tofu, drained and pressed
- 1/2 cup flour
- 2 tablespoons cornstarch
- 1/2 teaspoon salt
- 1/4 teaspoon black pepper
- 1/2 cup shredded coconut
- 1/4 cup unsweetened coconut flakes
- 1/2 cup water
- Vegetable oil for frying

Instructions:

1. Cut the tofu into cubes or slabs. In a shallow bowl, combine flour, cornstarch, salt, and pepper.
2. In another shallow bowl, mix the shredded coconut and coconut flakes.
3. Dip each tofu piece into the flour mixture, then into the water, and finally coat with the coconut mixture.
4. Heat oil in a frying pan over medium heat. Fry the tofu for 3-4 minutes per side until golden brown and crispy.
5. Drain on paper towels and serve with a dipping sauce of your choice.

Coconut Rice Pudding

Ingredients:

- 1 cup Arborio rice (or short-grain rice)
- 1 can (14 oz) coconut milk
- 1 1/2 cups milk
- 1/2 cup sugar
- 1/2 teaspoon vanilla extract
- 1/4 teaspoon salt
- Ground cinnamon for garnish

Instructions:

1. In a saucepan, combine rice, coconut milk, milk, sugar, and salt. Bring to a simmer over medium heat.
2. Stir the mixture occasionally, cooking for 20-25 minutes until the rice is tender and the pudding has thickened.
3. Remove from heat and stir in vanilla extract.
4. Serve warm or chilled, garnished with ground cinnamon.

Coconut Shrimp Tacos

Ingredients:

- 1 lb shrimp, peeled and deveined
- 1/2 cup shredded coconut
- 1/2 cup panko breadcrumbs
- 1 egg, beaten
- 1/2 teaspoon chili powder
- 1/4 teaspoon cumin
- 1 tablespoon vegetable oil
- Small tortillas
- Cabbage slaw (optional)
- Lime wedges
- Cilantro for garnish

Instructions:

1. Preheat the oven to 400°F (200°C). Mix shredded coconut and panko breadcrumbs with chili powder and cumin in a shallow bowl.
2. Dip each shrimp into the beaten egg, then coat in the coconut-breadcrumb mixture.
3. Heat oil in a skillet over medium heat. Cook the shrimp for 2-3 minutes on each side until golden brown and crispy.
4. Warm tortillas and fill with shrimp, cabbage slaw, and garnish with cilantro and lime wedges.

Thai Coconut Soup (Tom Kha Gai)

Ingredients:

- 1 lb chicken breast, sliced thinly
- 1 can (14 oz) coconut milk
- 3 cups chicken broth
- 2 stalks lemongrass, smashed
- 4-5 kaffir lime leaves, torn
- 3-4 slices fresh galangal or ginger
- 2-3 Thai bird chilies, smashed
- 1 tablespoon fish sauce
- 1 tablespoon sugar
- 1 tablespoon lime juice
- Fresh cilantro for garnish

Instructions:

1. In a large pot, combine chicken broth, coconut milk, lemongrass, kaffir lime leaves, galangal, and chilies. Bring to a boil.
2. Add the chicken slices and simmer for 10-12 minutes until the chicken is cooked.
3. Stir in fish sauce, sugar, and lime juice. Taste and adjust seasoning if needed.
4. Garnish with fresh cilantro and serve hot.

Coconut and Lime Chicken Skewers

Ingredients:

- 1 lb chicken breast, cut into cubes
- 1/2 cup coconut milk
- Zest and juice of 1 lime
- 2 cloves garlic, minced
- 1 tablespoon soy sauce
- 1 tablespoon honey
- 1 teaspoon ground cumin
- 1/2 teaspoon ground turmeric
- Salt and pepper to taste
- Bamboo skewers

Instructions:

1. In a bowl, combine coconut milk, lime zest and juice, garlic, soy sauce, honey, cumin, turmeric, salt, and pepper.
2. Add the chicken cubes and marinate for at least 30 minutes.
3. Thread the chicken onto bamboo skewers.
4. Grill over medium heat for 5-7 minutes per side until the chicken is cooked through.
5. Serve the skewers with additional lime wedges and cilantro.

Coconut Cream Pie

Ingredients:

- 1 pre-baked pie crust (9-inch)
- 1 can (14 oz) coconut milk
- 1 cup heavy cream
- 1/2 cup sugar
- 1/4 cup cornstarch
- 1/4 teaspoon salt
- 4 large egg yolks
- 1 teaspoon vanilla extract
- 1 cup shredded coconut (sweetened or unsweetened)
- Whipped cream for topping

Instructions:

1. In a medium saucepan, combine coconut milk, heavy cream, sugar, cornstarch, and salt. Heat over medium heat, stirring constantly until it begins to thicken.
2. In a bowl, whisk the egg yolks. Slowly pour some of the hot mixture into the egg yolks, then return the egg mixture to the saucepan.
3. Stir the mixture and cook for another 2-3 minutes until thickened. Remove from heat and stir in vanilla extract and shredded coconut.
4. Pour the filling into the pre-baked pie crust and smooth the top. Let it cool at room temperature for 30 minutes, then refrigerate for at least 2 hours.
5. Top with whipped cream before serving.

Coconut Avocado Salad

Ingredients:

- 1 avocado, diced
- 1/2 cup shredded coconut (unsweetened)
- 1 cucumber, sliced
- 1/4 red onion, thinly sliced
- 1 tablespoon fresh cilantro, chopped
- Juice of 1 lime
- Salt and pepper to taste

Instructions:

1. In a large bowl, combine diced avocado, shredded coconut, cucumber, red onion, and cilantro.
2. Drizzle with lime juice and season with salt and pepper.
3. Toss gently and serve immediately.

Coconut Banana Pancakes

Ingredients:

- 1 cup all-purpose flour
- 1/2 cup shredded coconut (unsweetened)
- 2 tablespoons sugar
- 1 tablespoon baking powder
- 1/2 teaspoon salt
- 1 cup coconut milk
- 1 egg
- 1 ripe banana, mashed
- 1 teaspoon vanilla extract
- Butter or oil for frying

Instructions:

1. In a bowl, combine flour, shredded coconut, sugar, baking powder, and salt.
2. In another bowl, whisk together coconut milk, egg, mashed banana, and vanilla extract.
3. Pour the wet ingredients into the dry ingredients and stir until combined.
4. Heat a griddle or frying pan over medium heat and lightly grease with butter or oil.
5. Pour the pancake batter onto the griddle and cook for 2-3 minutes per side until golden brown. Serve with maple syrup or fresh fruit.

Coconut-Lime Grilled Salmon

Ingredients:

- 4 salmon fillets
- 1/4 cup coconut milk
- Juice and zest of 1 lime
- 2 tablespoons olive oil
- 1 tablespoon honey
- 2 cloves garlic, minced
- Salt and pepper to taste
- Fresh cilantro for garnish

Instructions:

1. In a bowl, whisk together coconut milk, lime juice and zest, olive oil, honey, garlic, salt, and pepper.
2. Pour the marinade over the salmon fillets and refrigerate for at least 30 minutes.
3. Preheat the grill to medium-high heat. Grill the salmon for 4-5 minutes per side, or until the fish flakes easily with a fork.
4. Garnish with fresh cilantro and serve.

Coconut-Curry Beef Stew

Ingredients:

- 1 lb beef stew meat, cubed
- 2 tablespoons vegetable oil
- 1 onion, chopped
- 2 cloves garlic, minced
- 1 tablespoon grated ginger
- 2 tablespoons red curry paste
- 1 can (14 oz) coconut milk
- 2 cups beef broth
- 1 carrot, sliced
- 1 potato, diced
- 1 tablespoon fish sauce
- 1 teaspoon turmeric
- 1/2 teaspoon cumin
- Salt and pepper to taste

Instructions:

1. Heat vegetable oil in a large pot over medium heat. Add the beef cubes and brown on all sides.
2. Add onions, garlic, and ginger, and cook for 2-3 minutes until softened.
3. Stir in red curry paste, coconut milk, beef broth, carrot, potato, fish sauce, turmeric, cumin, salt, and pepper.
4. Bring to a simmer, then reduce heat and cook for 1-1.5 hours until the beef is tender and the stew has thickened.
5. Serve with rice or crusty bread.

Coconut Almond Macaroons

Ingredients:

- 2 1/2 cups shredded coconut (unsweetened)
- 1/2 cup almond meal
- 1/4 cup sugar
- 2 large egg whites
- 1 teaspoon vanilla extract
- Pinch of salt
- 1/4 cup sliced almonds (optional)

Instructions:

1. Preheat the oven to 325°F (165°C). Line a baking sheet with parchment paper.
2. In a bowl, combine shredded coconut, almond meal, sugar, egg whites, vanilla extract, and salt. Stir until well combined.
3. Scoop tablespoon-sized portions of the mixture onto the baking sheet. If desired, top with a few sliced almonds.
4. Bake for 18-20 minutes until the macaroons are golden brown.
5. Let cool on the baking sheet before serving.

Coconut-Sesame Grilled Scallops

Ingredients:

- 1 lb scallops, cleaned and patted dry
- 2 tablespoons coconut oil, melted
- 1 tablespoon sesame oil
- 1 tablespoon soy sauce
- 1 tablespoon honey
- 1 teaspoon grated ginger
- 1 tablespoon sesame seeds
- Lime wedges for serving

Instructions:

1. In a bowl, whisk together coconut oil, sesame oil, soy sauce, honey, and ginger.
2. Add the scallops to the bowl and toss to coat. Marinate for 15-20 minutes.
3. Preheat the grill to medium-high heat. Grill the scallops for 2-3 minutes per side until golden brown and cooked through.
4. Sprinkle with sesame seeds and serve with lime wedges.

Coconut-Chocolate Truffles

Ingredients:

- 1 cup dark chocolate chips
- 1/2 cup coconut milk
- 1/2 teaspoon vanilla extract
- 1 cup shredded coconut (unsweetened)
- 1 tablespoon honey

Instructions:

1. In a saucepan, heat coconut milk over medium heat until it begins to simmer.
2. Remove from heat and add the chocolate chips, stirring until melted and smooth.
3. Stir in vanilla extract and honey.
4. Let the mixture cool for 10 minutes, then refrigerate for 1 hour or until firm enough to roll into balls.
5. Roll the truffles into small balls and coat in shredded coconut.
6. Refrigerate again until firm, and serve chilled.

Coconut Sweet Potato Soup

Ingredients:

- 2 medium sweet potatoes, peeled and diced
- 1 can (14 oz) coconut milk
- 1 onion, chopped
- 2 cloves garlic, minced
- 1 teaspoon grated ginger
- 4 cups vegetable broth
- 1 teaspoon cumin
- Salt and pepper to taste
- Fresh cilantro for garnish

Instructions:

1. Heat a pot over medium heat. Add onion, garlic, and ginger, and sauté for 5-7 minutes until softened.
2. Add the diced sweet potatoes, coconut milk, vegetable broth, cumin, salt, and pepper.
3. Bring to a boil, then reduce the heat and simmer for 20-25 minutes until the sweet potatoes are tender.
4. Use an immersion blender to puree the soup until smooth, or transfer to a blender in batches.
5. Garnish with fresh cilantro and serve.

Coconut Yogurt Parfait

Ingredients:

- 1 cup coconut yogurt
- 1/2 cup granola
- 1/4 cup shredded coconut
- 1/2 cup mixed berries (strawberries, blueberries, raspberries)
- 1 tbsp honey (optional)

Instructions:

1. In a glass or bowl, layer coconut yogurt, granola, and shredded coconut.
2. Add a layer of mixed berries on top.
3. Drizzle with honey if desired.
4. Repeat the layers as desired and finish with a top layer of berries and coconut.
5. Serve immediately or chill for later.

Coconut Milk Ice Cream

Ingredients:

- 2 cans (14 oz each) coconut milk
- 1/2 cup sugar (or sweetener of choice)
- 1 tsp vanilla extract
- A pinch of salt

Instructions:

1. In a medium saucepan, combine the coconut milk, sugar, and a pinch of salt.
2. Heat over medium heat, stirring until the sugar is dissolved.
3. Remove from heat and stir in vanilla extract.
4. Allow the mixture to cool to room temperature, then refrigerate for at least 4 hours.
5. Once chilled, churn the mixture in an ice cream maker according to the manufacturer's instructions.
6. Once churned, transfer to an airtight container and freeze for at least 2 hours before serving.

Coconut-Rice Stuffed Peppers

Ingredients:

- 4 bell peppers, tops cut off and seeds removed
- 1 cup cooked rice (preferably jasmine or basmati)
- 1/2 cup shredded coconut
- 1/4 cup chopped cilantro
- 1/2 cup coconut milk
- 1 small onion, chopped
- 1 garlic clove, minced
- 1/2 tsp cumin
- 1/2 tsp turmeric
- Salt and pepper to taste

Instructions:

1. Preheat the oven to 375°F (190°C).
2. In a skillet, sauté the onion and garlic in a little oil until softened.
3. Add the cooked rice, shredded coconut, cilantro, coconut milk, cumin, turmeric, salt, and pepper. Stir well to combine and heat through.
4. Stuff the bell peppers with the rice mixture and place them in a baking dish.
5. Cover with foil and bake for 30 minutes.
6. Uncover and bake for an additional 10 minutes, until the peppers are tender.
7. Serve with additional cilantro if desired.

Coconut-Cashew Chicken Stir-Fry

Ingredients:

- 2 chicken breasts, sliced into thin strips
- 1/2 cup cashews
- 1/2 cup coconut milk
- 1 tbsp soy sauce
- 1 tbsp honey
- 1 tsp garlic, minced
- 1 tbsp ginger, minced
- 2 tbsp coconut oil
- 1 bell pepper, sliced
- 1 onion, sliced
- 2 cups broccoli florets
- Salt and pepper to taste

Instructions:

1. Heat coconut oil in a large pan over medium heat. Add the chicken strips and cook until browned and cooked through. Remove from the pan and set aside.
2. In the same pan, add the garlic, ginger, bell pepper, onion, and broccoli. Stir-fry for 4-5 minutes until the vegetables are tender.
3. Add the coconut milk, soy sauce, and honey to the pan. Stir well to combine.
4. Add the chicken back to the pan along with the cashews. Stir everything together and cook for an additional 2-3 minutes until heated through.
5. Season with salt and pepper, and serve over rice.

Coconut-Maple Granola

Ingredients:

- 2 cups rolled oats
- 1/2 cup shredded coconut
- 1/4 cup maple syrup
- 1/4 cup coconut oil, melted
- 1/2 tsp vanilla extract
- 1/4 tsp salt
- 1/2 cup chopped nuts (almonds, cashews, or walnuts)
- 1/4 cup dried fruit (raisins, cranberries, etc.)

Instructions:

1. Preheat the oven to 350°F (175°C).
2. In a large bowl, combine oats, shredded coconut, maple syrup, melted coconut oil, vanilla extract, and salt.
3. Spread the mixture evenly on a baking sheet and bake for 20-25 minutes, stirring halfway through, until golden brown.
4. Remove from the oven and allow to cool completely.
5. Stir in the chopped nuts and dried fruit.
6. Store in an airtight container for up to two weeks.

Coconut Cabbage Slaw

Ingredients:

- 4 cups shredded cabbage (green or purple)
- 1/2 cup shredded coconut
- 1/4 cup rice vinegar
- 2 tbsp coconut oil
- 1 tbsp honey
- 1/2 tsp mustard powder
- Salt and pepper to taste

Instructions:

1. In a large bowl, combine the shredded cabbage and shredded coconut.
2. In a separate bowl, whisk together rice vinegar, coconut oil, honey, mustard powder, salt, and pepper.
3. Pour the dressing over the cabbage mixture and toss to coat evenly.
4. Let the slaw sit for 15-20 minutes to allow the flavors to meld.
5. Serve as a side dish or topping for tacos or grilled meats.

Coconut and Mango Chutney

Ingredients:

- 1 ripe mango, peeled and diced
- 1/2 cup shredded coconut
- 1/4 cup apple cider vinegar
- 1/4 cup brown sugar
- 1/4 tsp ground ginger
- 1/4 tsp ground cinnamon
- 1/4 tsp ground cloves
- 1/4 tsp mustard seeds (optional)
- Pinch of salt

Instructions:

1. In a saucepan, combine mango, shredded coconut, apple cider vinegar, brown sugar, ginger, cinnamon, cloves, mustard seeds (if using), and salt.
2. Cook over medium heat, stirring occasionally, for about 20-25 minutes, until the mixture thickens.
3. Remove from heat and let cool.
4. Store in an airtight jar in the fridge for up to two weeks.
5. Serve with grilled meats, curries, or as a condiment for sandwiches.

Coconut-Lime Bars

Ingredients:

- 1 cup shredded coconut
- 1/2 cup coconut flour
- 1/4 cup coconut oil, melted
- 2 tbsp maple syrup
- 1/2 tsp vanilla extract
- Zest and juice of 2 limes
- 2 large eggs
- 1/4 cup honey
- Pinch of salt

Instructions:

1. Preheat the oven to 350°F (175°C). Grease a baking dish with coconut oil.
2. In a bowl, combine shredded coconut, coconut flour, melted coconut oil, maple syrup, vanilla extract, lime zest, and lime juice. Mix until well combined.
3. In another bowl, whisk together the eggs, honey, and a pinch of salt.
4. Pour the egg mixture into the coconut mixture and stir to combine.
5. Pour the batter into the prepared baking dish and bake for 20-25 minutes, until set and golden.
6. Allow the bars to cool completely before cutting into squares.
7. Serve as a refreshing, tangy dessert.

Coconut-Peanut Butter Smoothie

Ingredients:

- 1 banana
- 1/2 cup coconut milk
- 2 tbsp peanut butter
- 1/4 cup shredded coconut
- 1 tbsp honey or maple syrup (optional)
- 1/2 cup ice

Instructions:

1. Add the banana, coconut milk, peanut butter, shredded coconut, and honey (if using) to a blender.
2. Blend until smooth, adding ice for thickness or more coconut milk to reach the desired consistency.
3. Pour into a glass and garnish with extra shredded coconut if desired.
4. Serve immediately and enjoy!

Coconut Creamed Spinach

Ingredients:

- 4 cups fresh spinach, washed and chopped
- 1/2 cup coconut milk
- 1/4 cup coconut cream
- 2 garlic cloves, minced
- 1/4 tsp nutmeg
- Salt and pepper to taste
- 1 tbsp olive oil

Instructions:

1. Heat olive oil in a large pan over medium heat. Add garlic and sauté until fragrant, about 1 minute.
2. Add the chopped spinach and cook until wilted, about 3-4 minutes.
3. Pour in the coconut milk and coconut cream, stirring to combine.
4. Season with nutmeg, salt, and pepper. Cook for an additional 2-3 minutes, allowing the mixture to thicken.
5. Serve warm as a delicious side dish.

Coconut-Curry Mussels

Ingredients:

- 2 lbs mussels, cleaned and debearded
- 1 tbsp coconut oil
- 1 small onion, finely chopped
- 2 garlic cloves, minced
- 1 tbsp grated ginger
- 1 tbsp red curry paste
- 1 cup coconut milk
- 1/4 cup fresh cilantro, chopped
- 1 tbsp lime juice
- Salt and pepper to taste

Instructions:

1. Heat coconut oil in a large pot over medium heat. Add onion, garlic, and ginger, sautéing until softened, about 5 minutes.
2. Stir in the red curry paste and cook for 1-2 minutes.
3. Pour in the coconut milk and bring to a simmer.
4. Add the mussels, cover the pot, and cook for 5-7 minutes until the mussels open.
5. Discard any mussels that do not open.
6. Stir in fresh cilantro and lime juice, and season with salt and pepper.
7. Serve with crusty bread to soak up the flavorful broth.

Coconut Panna Cotta

Ingredients:

- 1 can (14 oz) coconut milk
- 1/2 cup heavy cream (or more coconut milk for a dairy-free version)
- 1/2 cup sugar
- 1 tsp vanilla extract
- 1 packet (2 1/4 tsp) gelatin
- 2 tbsp water

Instructions:

1. In a small bowl, sprinkle gelatin over 2 tbsp of water. Let it sit for 5-10 minutes to bloom.
2. In a saucepan, combine coconut milk, heavy cream, and sugar. Heat over medium heat, stirring occasionally, until the sugar dissolves.
3. Remove from heat and stir in the vanilla extract.
4. Add the bloomed gelatin to the mixture, stirring until completely dissolved.
5. Pour the panna cotta mixture into molds or glasses and refrigerate for at least 4 hours, or overnight, until set.
6. Serve chilled, optionally with fresh fruit or a drizzle of caramel sauce.

Coconut Date Energy Balls

Ingredients:

- 1 cup medjool dates, pitted
- 1/2 cup shredded coconut
- 1/4 cup almond butter
- 1 tbsp coconut oil
- 1/4 cup rolled oats
- 1/4 tsp vanilla extract
- 1/4 tsp salt

Instructions:

1. In a food processor, pulse the dates until finely chopped.
2. Add the shredded coconut, almond butter, coconut oil, oats, vanilla extract, and salt. Pulse until the mixture comes together and forms a sticky dough.
3. Roll the mixture into small balls, about 1 inch in diameter.
4. If desired, roll the balls in extra shredded coconut for a coating.
5. Refrigerate for at least 30 minutes before serving.
6. Store in an airtight container in the fridge for up to a week.

Coconut-Curry Hummus

Ingredients:

- 1 can (15 oz) chickpeas, drained and rinsed
- 1/2 cup coconut milk
- 1 tbsp tahini
- 1 tbsp curry powder
- 1 garlic clove, minced
- 1/2 tsp ground cumin
- 1/4 tsp ground turmeric
- Salt and pepper to taste
- 1 tbsp olive oil

Instructions:

1. In a food processor, combine chickpeas, coconut milk, tahini, curry powder, garlic, cumin, turmeric, salt, and pepper.
2. Blend until smooth, scraping down the sides as needed.
3. Drizzle in olive oil and blend again until creamy.
4. Adjust seasoning if needed and serve with pita, crackers, or veggies.
5. Store in an airtight container in the fridge for up to 5 days.

Coconut Shrimp with Pineapple Salsa

Ingredients:

- 1 lb large shrimp, peeled and deveined
- 1/2 cup shredded coconut
- 1/4 cup flour
- 1 egg, beaten
- 1/2 tsp paprika
- 1/4 tsp cayenne pepper
- Salt and pepper to taste
- 2 tbsp coconut oil for frying

For the Pineapple Salsa:

- 1 cup fresh pineapple, diced
- 1/4 red onion, diced
- 1/4 cup cilantro, chopped
- 1 tbsp lime juice
- Salt and pepper to taste

Instructions:

1. In a shallow bowl, combine shredded coconut, flour, paprika, cayenne, salt, and pepper.
2. Dip each shrimp in the beaten egg, then coat with the coconut mixture.
3. Heat coconut oil in a large pan over medium heat. Fry shrimp for 2-3 minutes on each side, until golden and crispy.
4. While shrimp cook, combine the pineapple, red onion, cilantro, lime juice, salt, and pepper in a small bowl to make the salsa.
5. Serve the coconut shrimp with a generous spoonful of pineapple salsa on top.

Coconut Chicken Skewers with Peanut Sauce

Ingredients:

- 2 chicken breasts, cut into cubes
- 1/2 cup shredded coconut
- 1/4 cup breadcrumbs
- 1/4 cup coconut milk
- 1 tbsp coconut oil
- 8-10 wooden skewers (soaked in water for 30 minutes)

For the Peanut Sauce:

- 1/4 cup peanut butter
- 2 tbsp soy sauce
- 1 tbsp honey
- 1 tbsp lime juice
- 1 tbsp sesame oil
- 1/4 cup water (to thin the sauce)

Instructions:

1. Preheat the grill to medium-high heat.
2. In a shallow dish, combine shredded coconut and breadcrumbs. Dip the chicken cubes into coconut milk, then coat them with the coconut-breadcrumb mixture.
3. Thread the coated chicken cubes onto the soaked skewers.
4. Grill the chicken skewers for 5-7 minutes on each side until cooked through.
5. While the chicken cooks, whisk together all peanut sauce ingredients in a small bowl, adding water to reach your desired consistency.
6. Serve the chicken skewers with peanut sauce for dipping.

Coconut Chocolate Cake

Ingredients:

- 1 cup all-purpose flour
- 1/2 cup unsweetened cocoa powder
- 1 tsp baking powder
- 1/2 tsp baking soda
- 1/4 tsp salt
- 1/2 cup coconut oil, melted
- 1 cup coconut sugar or brown sugar
- 2 large eggs
- 1 tsp vanilla extract
- 1/2 cup coconut milk
- 1/2 cup shredded coconut (for garnish)

Instructions:

1. Preheat the oven to 350°F (175°C). Grease and flour an 8-inch round cake pan.
2. In a bowl, sift together the flour, cocoa powder, baking powder, baking soda, and salt.
3. In a separate bowl, whisk together the melted coconut oil, coconut sugar, eggs, and vanilla extract until smooth.
4. Gradually add the dry ingredients to the wet ingredients, alternating with the coconut milk. Stir until combined.
5. Pour the batter into the prepared cake pan and smooth the top.
6. Bake for 30-35 minutes, or until a toothpick inserted into the center comes out clean.
7. Let the cake cool completely before removing it from the pan.
8. Garnish with shredded coconut and serve.

Coconut-Banana Smoothie

Ingredients:

- 1 ripe banana
- 1/2 cup coconut milk
- 1/2 cup plain yogurt (or coconut yogurt for a dairy-free version)
- 1 tbsp honey or maple syrup
- 1/4 tsp cinnamon
- Ice cubes (optional)

Instructions:

1. In a blender, combine the banana, coconut milk, yogurt, honey, and cinnamon.
2. Blend until smooth, adding ice cubes for extra chill, if desired.
3. Pour into a glass and serve immediately.

Coconut Milk Risotto with Shrimp

Ingredients:

- 1 cup Arborio rice
- 1 can (14 oz) coconut milk
- 1 1/2 cups chicken or vegetable broth
- 1/2 lb shrimp, peeled and deveined
- 1/2 small onion, finely chopped
- 2 garlic cloves, minced
- 1 tbsp coconut oil
- 1/4 cup grated Parmesan cheese (optional)
- Salt and pepper to taste
- Fresh cilantro or parsley for garnish

Instructions:

1. Heat coconut oil in a large pan over medium heat. Add the onion and garlic, cooking until softened, about 2-3 minutes.
2. Stir in the Arborio rice and cook for 1-2 minutes until the rice is lightly toasted.
3. Gradually add the coconut milk and broth, 1/2 cup at a time, stirring constantly until the liquid is absorbed before adding more.
4. Continue until the rice is creamy and cooked through, about 20 minutes.
5. While the risotto is cooking, heat a separate pan over medium heat and cook the shrimp for 2-3 minutes on each side until pink and opaque.
6. Stir the cooked shrimp into the risotto, and season with salt, pepper, and Parmesan cheese if desired.
7. Garnish with fresh cilantro or parsley and serve warm.

Coconut Creamed Corn

Ingredients:

- 4 cups fresh or frozen corn kernels
- 1/2 cup coconut milk
- 1/4 cup coconut cream
- 2 tbsp butter or coconut oil
- 1/2 tsp garlic powder
- Salt and pepper to taste
- Fresh parsley or cilantro for garnish

Instructions:

1. In a large pan, melt the butter or coconut oil over medium heat.
2. Add the corn and cook for 5-7 minutes until tender.
3. Pour in the coconut milk and coconut cream, stirring to combine.
4. Season with garlic powder, salt, and pepper. Simmer for 3-5 minutes until heated through and creamy.
5. Garnish with fresh parsley or cilantro and serve warm.

Coconut-Chicken Satay

Ingredients:

- 1 lb chicken breast, cut into strips
- 1/2 cup coconut milk
- 2 tbsp soy sauce
- 1 tbsp lime juice
- 1 tbsp brown sugar
- 1 tsp ground turmeric
- 1/2 tsp ground cumin
- 1/2 tsp chili powder
- 1 tbsp coconut oil (for grilling)

For the Peanut Sauce:

- 1/4 cup peanut butter
- 2 tbsp soy sauce
- 1 tbsp lime juice
- 1 tbsp honey
- 1/4 cup coconut milk
- 1/2 tsp ground ginger

Instructions:

1. In a bowl, combine coconut milk, soy sauce, lime juice, brown sugar, turmeric, cumin, and chili powder.
2. Add the chicken strips to the marinade, toss to coat, and refrigerate for at least 30 minutes.
3. Preheat a grill or grill pan over medium heat.
4. Thread the marinated chicken onto skewers and grill for 5-7 minutes on each side, until cooked through.
5. While the chicken is cooking, whisk together the peanut butter, soy sauce, lime juice, honey, coconut milk, and ground ginger in a small bowl.
6. Serve the chicken satay with the peanut sauce on the side.

Coconut-Peanut Stir-Fried Noodles

Ingredients:

- 8 oz rice noodles
- 1/2 cup coconut milk
- 2 tbsp peanut butter
- 1 tbsp soy sauce
- 1 tbsp lime juice
- 1 tbsp brown sugar
- 1/2 tsp chili flakes (optional)
- 1/2 cup shredded carrots
- 1/2 red bell pepper, sliced
- 1 tbsp coconut oil
- Fresh cilantro for garnish

Instructions:

1. Cook the rice noodles according to package instructions. Drain and set aside.
2. In a small bowl, whisk together coconut milk, peanut butter, soy sauce, lime juice, brown sugar, and chili flakes until smooth.
3. Heat coconut oil in a pan over medium heat. Add the shredded carrots and bell pepper, sautéing for 2-3 minutes until softened.
4. Add the cooked noodles to the pan and pour the coconut-peanut sauce over the top. Toss to coat the noodles evenly.
5. Cook for an additional 2-3 minutes to heat through.
6. Garnish with fresh cilantro and serve warm.

Coconut-Pumpkin Soup

Ingredients:

- 2 cups pumpkin puree
- 1 can (14 oz) coconut milk
- 1/2 cup vegetable broth
- 1 small onion, chopped
- 2 garlic cloves, minced
- 1/2 tsp ground ginger
- 1/4 tsp ground cinnamon
- 1/4 tsp ground nutmeg
- Salt and pepper to taste
- 1 tbsp coconut oil

Instructions:

1. Heat coconut oil in a large pot over medium heat. Add the onion and garlic, cooking until softened, about 3-4 minutes.
2. Stir in the pumpkin puree, coconut milk, and vegetable broth.
3. Add the ginger, cinnamon, nutmeg, salt, and pepper. Bring the soup to a simmer and cook for 10-15 minutes, stirring occasionally.
4. Use an immersion blender to blend the soup until smooth (or transfer in batches to a blender).
5. Taste and adjust seasoning if needed. Serve warm.

Coconut-Cilantro Rice

Ingredients:

- 1 cup basmati rice
- 1 can (14 oz) coconut milk
- 1/2 cup water
- 1/2 tsp salt
- 1/4 cup fresh cilantro, chopped

Instructions:

1. In a medium saucepan, combine rice, coconut milk, water, and salt.
2. Bring to a boil, then reduce the heat to low, cover, and simmer for 18-20 minutes until the rice is tender and the liquid is absorbed.
3. Remove from heat and let it sit, covered, for 5 minutes.
4. Fluff the rice with a fork and stir in the chopped cilantro.
5. Serve as a side dish with your favorite meal.

Coconut-Rosemary Lamb Chops

Ingredients:

- 4 lamb chops (about 1 inch thick)
- 1/2 cup shredded coconut (unsweetened)
- 2 tablespoons fresh rosemary, finely chopped
- 2 tablespoons olive oil
- 1 tablespoon Dijon mustard
- 1 tablespoon honey
- 1/2 teaspoon garlic powder
- Salt and pepper, to taste
- Lemon wedges, for serving

Instructions:

1. **Prepare the Marinade:** In a small bowl, whisk together the olive oil, Dijon mustard, honey, garlic powder, chopped rosemary, salt, and pepper.
2. **Marinate the Lamb:** Place the lamb chops in a shallow dish or a resealable bag. Pour the marinade over the lamb, making sure each chop is well-coated. Refrigerate for at least 1 hour or up to overnight for maximum flavor.
3. **Prepare the Coconut Coating:** Spread the shredded coconut in a shallow dish. Once the lamb chops have marinated, remove them from the dish and press each chop into the coconut, ensuring they are evenly coated on all sides.
4. **Cook the Lamb:** Heat a large skillet or grill pan over medium-high heat. Add a drizzle of olive oil to the pan. Once hot, add the lamb chops and cook for 3-4 minutes per side for medium-rare, or longer to your preferred doneness.
5. **Serve:** Transfer the lamb chops to a plate and let them rest for a few minutes. Serve with fresh lemon wedges on the side for an added burst of flavor.

Coconut Mousse with Raspberries

Ingredients:

- 1 can (14 oz) coconut milk
- 1/2 cup heavy cream
- 1/4 cup powdered sugar
- 1 teaspoon vanilla extract
- 1/2 teaspoon coconut extract
- 1/2 cup fresh raspberries
- Toasted coconut flakes, for garnish

Instructions:

1. In a mixing bowl, combine coconut milk, heavy cream, powdered sugar, vanilla extract, and coconut extract. Whisk until smooth.
2. Refrigerate for 1 hour to allow the mousse to set.
3. Spoon the mousse into serving glasses. Top with fresh raspberries and toasted coconut flakes.
4. Serve chilled and enjoy.

Coconut Rice with Mango and Chia

Ingredients:

- 1 cup jasmine rice
- 1 can (14 oz) coconut milk
- 1 cup water
- 1 tablespoon chia seeds
- 1 ripe mango, peeled and diced
- 1 tablespoon honey or maple syrup
- Pinch of salt

Instructions:

1. In a saucepan, combine rice, coconut milk, water, and a pinch of salt. Bring to a boil.
2. Reduce heat, cover, and simmer for 18-20 minutes, or until rice is tender.
3. Stir in chia seeds and honey/maple syrup. Let the mixture sit for 5 minutes.
4. Top the rice with diced mango and serve warm.

Coconut and Spinach Frittata

Ingredients:

- 6 large eggs
- 1/2 cup coconut milk
- 1 cup fresh spinach, chopped
- 1/2 cup shredded coconut
- 1/4 cup grated Parmesan cheese
- 1 tablespoon olive oil
- Salt and pepper, to taste

Instructions:

1. Preheat the oven to 375°F (190°C).
2. In a bowl, whisk together eggs, coconut milk, Parmesan cheese, salt, and pepper.
3. Heat olive oil in an oven-safe skillet over medium heat. Add spinach and cook until wilted.
4. Pour the egg mixture into the skillet, stirring to combine with the spinach.
5. Sprinkle shredded coconut on top and transfer the skillet to the oven.
6. Bake for 15-20 minutes or until set. Serve warm.

Coconut Pineapple Rice

Ingredients:

- 1 cup basmati rice
- 1 can (14 oz) coconut milk
- 1/2 cup pineapple chunks (fresh or canned)
- 1/2 cup water
- 1 tablespoon coconut oil
- Salt to taste

Instructions:

1. Rinse rice under cold water until water runs clear.
2. In a saucepan, combine coconut milk, water, and salt. Bring to a boil.
3. Stir in the rice and reduce heat to a simmer. Cover and cook for 15-18 minutes.
4. Add pineapple chunks and coconut oil to the rice, and gently stir.
5. Serve warm as a side dish.

Coconut-Chocolate Chip Cookies

Ingredients:

- 1 1/2 cups all-purpose flour
- 1/2 cup shredded coconut
- 1/2 teaspoon baking soda
- 1/2 cup butter, softened
- 1/2 cup brown sugar
- 1/4 cup granulated sugar
- 1 large egg
- 1 teaspoon vanilla extract
- 1 cup chocolate chips

Instructions:

1. Preheat the oven to 350°F (175°C).
2. In a bowl, whisk together flour, shredded coconut, and baking soda.
3. In another bowl, cream together butter, brown sugar, and granulated sugar until light and fluffy.
4. Beat in the egg and vanilla extract. Gradually add the dry ingredients.
5. Stir in chocolate chips.
6. Drop tablespoon-sized balls of dough onto a baking sheet. Bake for 10-12 minutes until golden brown. Let cool on a wire rack.

Coconut Baked Cod with Lime

Ingredients:

- 4 cod fillets
- 1 cup shredded coconut
- 1/2 cup breadcrumbs
- 1 tablespoon olive oil
- 1 tablespoon lime juice
- Salt and pepper, to taste

Instructions:

1. Preheat the oven to 400°F (200°C).
2. In a shallow dish, combine shredded coconut, breadcrumbs, lime juice, salt, and pepper.
3. Brush cod fillets with olive oil and coat them in the coconut mixture.
4. Place the fillets on a baking sheet and bake for 12-15 minutes until the fish is cooked through and golden brown.
5. Serve with lime wedges.

Coconut-Lavender Scones

Ingredients:

- 2 cups all-purpose flour
- 1/4 cup shredded coconut
- 1 tablespoon dried lavender flowers
- 1/4 cup sugar
- 1 tablespoon baking powder
- 1/2 teaspoon salt
- 1/2 cup butter, cold and cubed
- 1/2 cup coconut milk
- 1 egg (for egg wash)

Instructions:

1. Preheat the oven to 375°F (190°C).
2. In a bowl, combine flour, sugar, baking powder, shredded coconut, and dried lavender.
3. Cut in the cold butter until the mixture resembles coarse crumbs.
4. Add coconut milk and stir until just combined.
5. Turn the dough onto a floured surface, shape into a circle, and cut into wedges.
6. Brush with egg wash and bake for 15-20 minutes until golden brown.

Coconut Lime Cheesecake

Ingredients:

- 1 1/2 cups graham cracker crumbs
- 1/2 cup shredded coconut
- 1/4 cup melted butter
- 3 (8 oz) packages cream cheese, softened
- 1 cup coconut milk
- 3/4 cup sugar
- 1 tablespoon lime zest
- 1/4 cup lime juice
- 3 large eggs

Instructions:

1. Preheat the oven to 325°F (160°C).
2. Mix graham cracker crumbs, shredded coconut, and melted butter. Press into the bottom of a springform pan.
3. In a bowl, beat cream cheese until smooth. Add coconut milk, sugar, lime zest, and lime juice. Mix until smooth.
4. Beat in the eggs one at a time.
5. Pour the mixture over the crust and bake for 50-60 minutes, or until the center is set.
6. Let cool completely, then refrigerate for at least 4 hours before serving.

www.ingramcontent.com/pod-product-compliance
Lightning Source LLC
LaVergne TN
LVHW081459060526
838201LV00056BA/2835